Bless your Spirit

Bless your Mind

Bless your Life

— Don B Byah:

D.B.B.

SEAS OF AFFIRMATION

Micro Poetry

Mystic Musings | Reasoned Reveries

Don Bo Byuti

nobody but I

PARTRIDGE

Copyright © 2021 by Don Bo Byuti.

ISBN: Hardcover   978-1-5437-6466-6
           Softcover   978-1-5437-6464-2
           eBook   978-1-5437-6465-9

All rights reserved. No part of this book may be used or reproduced by any means, graphic, electronic, or mechanical, including photocopying, recording, taping or by any information storage retrieval system without the written permission of the author except in the case of brief quotations embodied in critical articles and reviews.

Because of the dynamic nature of the Internet, any web addresses or links contained in this book may have changed since publication and may no longer be valid. The views expressed in this work are solely those of the author and do not necessarily reflect the views of the publisher, and the publisher hereby disclaims any responsibility for them.

Print information available on the last page.

To order additional copies of this book, contact
Toll Free +65 3165 7531 (Singapore)
Toll Free +60 3 3099 4412 (Malaysia)
orders.singapore@partridgepublishing.com

www.partridgepublishing.com/singapore

let's connect:
find me on Gab & Instagram

gab.com/poetofgab
instagram.com/don_bo_byuti

to Nova Rae & Veda Eve

*"Half of what
I say is meaningless;
but I say it so that
the other half
may reach
you"*
-Kahlil Gibran

*o' mystic moths
illuminated by faith be
resurrected in the light of unity
now unto tomorrow everlasting*

*all I've sought to achieve
in disquieting times as these
is to provide thy mind reprieve
from the tumult of gnashing teeth
by all the forces who wax supreme
attempting to subvert thy inner peace*

OM
O' Word
O' Logos
O' Primal Will
O' Absolute Truth
to Thee all souls sing
for Thee all spirits swoon
by Thee all creatures breathe
in Thee all creation communes
do lead us unto what draweth nigh
our hearts before Thy rapturous Light
O' Endless One
O' Supreme Lord
O' Love Glorified!

shanti
shalom
salaam
salutations
from a spiritual wayfarer
in a spiritually wayward nation

1

notice:
we may never see eye to eye
nor our convictions coincide
but may we stand alongside
one another ever dignified
in the timeless noble fight
to fortify the sacred right
of all to speak their mind
forthright

...

we can only make
one another think
awakening is free
free to wake or sleep
to be or not to be
there is only but to do
create what you say
first ask
who
are
you?

2

accept the challenge
of challenging the accepted

...

you must break from
in order to break through
but before any breakthrough
old paradigms need be subdued
rewired anew to
a new you

...

once
an unknown
is made known
one cannot not know
nor delete and let go
one can only accept it
and do the best with
the once unknown
newly made
known

3

the purpose to suffering
is to suffer for a purpose

...

the answer you desire
is answered in your desire

...

the truth you seek
is only found by truly seeking

...

the reason you're needing
is in your need for a reason

...

the meaning of struggling
is the struggle for meaning

4

we've been trained to think
we're wretched and weak

...

we've been beguiled into the belief
there's no need for belief

...

we've been conformed to conditions
designed to devour our spirits

...

may we see
that to assuredly see
know thyself we all first need
by sailing away from negation's bay
into the merciful breeze of a welcoming sea
while flowing auspiciously atop spiritual waves
under celestial guidance in affirmations embraced

5

veiled in
the most hidden of words
the spirit unveils
and souls affirm
that which *can't*
be read nor
heard

...

truth
{one must strive}
is never advertised
{to see between}
nor popularized
{the lines}

...

understand
you *won't* always
understand

6

missed will be
heaven's signs
till one elects to see
through heavenly eyes

...

the spirit
can never reign
till all brainwashing's
are washed from
the brain

...

what will
the children think
when they learn
they've been programmed
what to believe
but not how
to think?

7

fear lies in lies told by minds
darkness a myth only absence of light
shadow tells mind be fearful and hide
spirit tells mind to seek out the light
light shows mind that fear is a lie
minds free of fear are a life freed alive
a life freed alive is a spirit untied
a spirit untied is awakening realized

...

to face a fear
you must first
make it appear

...

feel more to fear less
from fearful to fearless

...

stand alone
if you *have* to
but stand firm is
what you *must* do

8

when we speak
through the spirit
only the spirit
in others can
hear it

...

everyone
becomes a teacher
to those who listen deeper

...

when we speak without speaking
we teach without teaching

...

one need not
comprehensively
comprehend the depths
to comprehend it has depth

9

knowledge
but without from
a multiplicity of sources
becomes stagnant universally

...

wisdom
but without from
a diversity of voices
becomes calcified internally

...

if you elect to
only see one color
or only eat one food
think of all the experiences
and opportunities that you'd
artificially limit yourself to

so it is for those of the opinion
to deny anything that doesn't fit within
the paradigms their pre-conceived notions insist

10

beauty is in the mind of the beholder
but the beauty of the beholder is the mind

...

beauty lived
but absent within
lives in denial
beauty within
but failed to lived
lives idle

...

there's more beauty in
a single cell from you and me
than in every ideology
taught at every
university

11

may you stay awake
even when asleep
so your dreams
become your
deeds

...

may you shatter your goals
instead of the promises
you promised your
soul

...

may you always
commit true vision
unto your projections
and in all ways heed
your spirit's candid
impressions

12

you can't outrun what's done
nor who you've let yourself become
you must face it or risk
facing repetition
ever endless

...

redemption
is of the One self
redeeming all selves
being but an incarnation
of Itself

...

until your faith
is sufficiently shaken
you will have yet
to sufficiently awaken

...

those who take
the leap of faith
soar with wings of
immeasurable grace

13

notice:
you must choose
what you're willing to lose
in the pursuits of novel truths

...

upon embracing
a new truth found
an old lie gets buried
six feet underground

...

if you haven't the heart to speak in truth
then why should ears ever be given
for listening to you?

...

everything beings
and ends with
a question

*so it is when
we pay attention*

14

may all soar
like moths unto
the Light of Truth
Whom transmutes
all spirits anew

...

clarity
will never feel as near and right
than it does when we mystic moths
in the misty maze of moonless night
find our way home to the Source of all Light

...

the whole point of mysticism
is for mystics to experience
wholeness mystically
within them

...

never have we *not*
been the same
yet we have yet
to *not* be different

15

the degree to which we each awaken
is determined by the angles taken
when escaping the cave to
sunlight's haven

...

the only thing
awakening can guarantee
is that the ability to let go
will come unnervingly easy

...

awakening is fruitless
if ego refuses to first confess
having been slumbering in hubris

...

realize:
not everyone
will awake in this life
no matter how hard you try
to expose their eyes to the light

16

free speech is hate speech
for those who hate
the right of *all*
to speak
freely

…

free speech defends
both freedom of dissent
and the right to freely offend

…

freedom forbids itself
from being forbidden
by the spoken word
and the will of
those whom
freely live

17

light without shadow is blind
shadow without light is confined

…

light in shadow
shadow in light
never isolated to one
but rather one intertwined

…

you must first conquer
your inner darkness
before you can harness
the Light of Providence
within the solace of
consciousness

…

affirm:
that you
will no longer
obscure your light
just to mollify another's
sensitive eyes

18

we're reminded by the swan
to not get bogged down
by the muck in
the pond

...

we're reminded by the crane
that without balance
all efforts perish
in vain

...

we're reminded by the koi fish
who swim in a circle
that reality is but
a flow eternal

...

we're reminded by the crow
who's judged so harshly
that life is as a story
of overcoming
past biases

19

perhaps to heal oneself personally
both emotionally and spiritually
is to heal one's cellular memory
from past ancestors and family trees
as if a choir singing together in jubilee
'we are free'

...

will you be the first in your family line
to mend the damages and rejuvenate the scars
scared over time?

...

some will use you
solely to use you
because it's just
what they do
but others
will attempt to use you
not because they mean to
but due to themselves being
so utterly used to being used
that they know not what they do

tis you who must see through the two

20

so much of how we
perceive and see
behave and grow
begins and ends
in the family
home

...

when a
child is given
full love and honor
by their mother *and* father
they won't have a need to pursue
remedies for cruel childhood abuse
in adults who experienced a similar youth
but who unconsciously inflict a familiar abuse

...

nothing defines you less
than what was forced
upon your person
before you had the ability
to form your own person

21

once you
begin to
see things
in a new light
the Light will
begin to
show you
new things

...

to stray too far from the light
is to render thy third eye inside blind

...

no one can have it all figured out
but everyone can have faith beyond all doubt

...

there is no benefit of the doubt
if all you do is doubt the benefits

22

how can
a spiritual war
amid ceaseless
psychological assaults
be categorically won
if a majority of
the targeted masses
have yet to accept
the war has even
begun?

...

the same ones who
offer up disingenuous remedies
wish us to be warring as enemies

...

cancerous personages orchestrate chaos
to foster for themselves a profitable payoff

23

notice:
if the end
is indeed here
then the beginning
is imminently near

...

how could we
not love one another
when each of us is but
a mirror of the other?

...

it's not the color of thy skin
but the extent that thine spirit
emanates from within

24

inner understanding must first root
before outer expanding can fully bloom

...

the more you come to know
the more solo to you'll tend go
the more at peace you'll be when alone

...

notice:
most people
perform their lives
as mimicking mimes
copying whatever they feel
is the most in vogue of the times

so it can be said
that a life of vicarious existence
is the individual's deepest dread

25

the most challenging decisions
challenge our most opinionated opinions
and cherished convictions

...

the best questions
are inherently destined
to have few answers
but many lessons

...

you shall
always wonder
what's the point
until you realize
that's the point

...

questions
are selections
by which we
navigate our
manifested
directions

26

mystics seek inwardness
propagandists seek conformists

...

disclosure pursues friendships
agendas pursue activists

...

uniqueness is privatized
obedience is commercialized

...

reason is understanding
indoctrination is demanding

...

awareness is the extent
that a reality can come to exist

27

from Oneness abundant
comes an abundance
of abundance

...

if what makes us different
bestows upon us our uniqueness
then only by sharing said differences
are we able to adequately fill up
all the space left available in
each of our unique cups
becoming the fullness
from whence all
oneness floods

...

divorce from any course
that *refuses* to endorse
Oneness as the Source

28

how much would your world change
if you made just the slightest change?

...

self-help only helps
the self that's willing to
help itself

...

where you're at
versus where you're headed
is manifested by mentality erected
through effort invested

...

if lust
is not tamed
it'll soon be wrath
and spiritual progress
will morph to shame
leaving you ashamed
of your selected path

29

enlightenment bears the burden
of becoming your own person

...

realize enlightenment
is not an attainment or achievement
but a realization realized in secret

...

the enlightened
use their enlightenment
to enlighten others on how to
arrive there without repeating
the same mistakes they did

...

affirm:
this life is it
you do not intend
on incarnating again
and when no choice is left
all that's left is enlightenment

30

Krishna is all
and all else is not
but a conscious thought
from Krishna's consciousness

…

Allah makes
the ethereal visible
and the celestial transmissible
amid the stillness of sentient syllables

…

layered into the labyrinths of life
are guidelines from Brahman
which all may come to find
on their path to realize
the Atman in
plain sight

31

if there were ever a risk worth taking
it's to risk oneself for another worth saving

so it is as
the Word infused
time to time to flesh
predestine to fulfill
a perennial mission
to illume all us dust
by reflecting the divine
and edifying all minds
while suffering unjustly
but doing so with serenity
as the ultimate sacrifice
paid for with fleshly life
from the cross at Calvary
to the courtyard in Tabriz
for all created things
seen and unseen
yet still so many
in our age today
insist on asking
are we actually
worth saving

what do you think?

32

The Word
and The Primal Point
as two sides of a single coin
exemplified for us nothing less
than the transcendent preeminence
of spiritual forbearance
especially
when confronted with
certain bodily death

it's the oldest story of humanity
that being the persecution
and barbaric execution
of those messengers closest
to transcendental holiness

...

dear embodied star
o' what a temple ye are
behold all marvel at the marble
the Primal Will forged for thy honor
so the timeless witness in thine heart may
behold a remembrance of thy spirit's blessedness

33

o' Illustrator of imagination
inseminating creative vibrations
by animating intuitions
with artistic visions

...

o' Master of unification
unifying all relations
by sanctifying salvation
in universal adoration

...

o' Orator of revelation
revealing enlightening emanations
by liberating thine creation
in the ways of spiritual
self-realization

34

o' Logos
o' Primal Point
all spirits are thine to awaken
all hearts are thine to point
towards the Sea of Affirmation
unto the Tree of Divine Unity
where fruits of fulfillment ripen
upon every branch and vine
from the nourishing utterances
of the Gospel's and
Bayan's voice so
forever sublime

...

ego is reactive
candor is passive
sorrow is stagnant
compassion a magnet
love is the magic
of heaven in action
as The Word of God
casts upon us spells
to shatter bad habits
to lead us to fresh wells
to emancipate our souls
from our personal hells

35

how can you witness what you're made of
if you hide from what you're afraid of?

...

you've already conquered earth
upon your conception and
survival from birth

...

even if
you can't always find it
know there always resides
a higher purpose
behind it

...

how can
some claim to
have higher principles
if they refuse to believe in
the presence of a higher Principle?

36

the best way to learn
is to question all you've learned

...

the more you choose to learn
the more you're forced to unlearn

...

the ones who unlearn to learn
learned the value of valuing their learnings

...

if you do not respect your mind
others will not mind disrespecting you

...

why sell your soul
just to do exactly
as you're told?

37

our errors shadow their corrections
our conclusions mirror our questions

...

an honest mistake is only so honest
in the honesty put forth towards
rectifying the results and
learning from the
mistake made

...

the prime directive towards correcting
any error or misapprehension
is first an acceptance of
the need for a
correction in
direction

38

what is goodness
without the bad?
can ease exist
without a difficult path?
can accomplishment live
without failure it's twin?
is sweetness even real
without knowing bitterness?
how could youth be seen
without also oldness?
could the future matter
if not for a past?
does first make sense
without the last?
perhaps
to recognize one
is to acknowledge its kin
perhaps then the key resides
in the mastery of balance
in the infinite present

Tao

39

today's most lethal condition
inhibiting spiritual vision
is too readily obeying
carnal conditioning's
conditions

...

a most costly phenomenon
of these phenomenal days
is believing at face value
what authoritarians convey
to suit their compulsions
for all ears to acquiesce
to their autocratic ways

...

overt social distancing
is just covert social conditioning

40

imagine if we
incinerated every field
upon an imperfect yield
every shrub or tree
upon a few rotten seeds
what would we leave
save the ashes of leaves
and a world left burning
from a utopian dream
to a dystopian scene

...

notice that the most intolerant
try and force the tolerant to repent
for crimes they didn't even commit

...

demoralization
by way of subversion
is a most insidious tactic
imposed upon unsuspecting persons
by those in power propagating
vast deceptions and
perversions

41

the waiting room
you wait in
waiting for
anything good to
happen to you
is akin to waiting
for the sun to shine
even though
you choose to
hide away inside
away from all light
blinds closed
doors bolted
pitch black
eyes blind

who knows what you'd see and find
if you only left that stagnant room behind
and made the most of your precious time

...

friction creates
cooperation sustains

42

there are times when
it's easier for a stranger
of open and impartial eyes
to behold your exceptional light
than it is for those who happen
to have known you for so long
yet have made up their minds
becoming numb to your shine
but do notice a situation as this
is only natural to witness
as it's effortless to take for granted
what we believe we already know
ergo
perhaps to perceive accurately
with piercing vision unabated
we must thoroughly inspect
the many views we hold
of those we closely know
but which have caused
our sight to be
blinded and
jaded

43

a most arduous task for the western mind
is removing the veil of duality
keeping minds confined
underneath unity divine

...

duality is a charade
disguising the reality
that undividedness pervades

...

to believe that consciousness
materializes from matter
is likewise to assume
candy is made by
its wrapper

...

to argue that
the whole of nature
has no intelligent creator
is akin to suggesting a tree
transforms itself into paper

44

who would have thought
the conflict of our times
for current and future lives
would be spiritually fought?
{spoiler alert}
all the sages
incarnations
manifestations
and prophets

...

the greatest rebellion
yet to fully unfold
is the battle for freeing
our minds and souls
from the clutches of those
wishing to see us
owned

...

the more hedonistic the music listened
the easier to deprave will be
the person listening

45

the mind
which neglects introspection
is as the explorer who rejects
a guide's direction

...

introspection sits
at the intersection
of inner reflection
and personal
confession

...

introspection
is to conscious meditation
what indoctrination
is to mental enslavement

...

isolation
inspires
introspection

46

there's nothing better for thy mental health
than remaining consciously vigilant
of thy immortal Self

...

self-realization
is actualized by the few who
master themselves
by transcending their
lower self

...

real wealth
is really felt
upon the recognition
of the real Self

...

offline
is the sublime
of modern times

47

resonate
with intention
as our every vibration
leaves a resounding indention

...

we may speak different languages
we may dwell in different nations
but we share the same vibrations

...

the alchemist
seeks not to change
mere copper to gold
but rather to disclose
the changeless
properties of
the soul

48

the more you listen
to your spirit yearn
the greater your soul
shall spiritually discern

...

to idolize the superficial
is to deify what's artificial

...

you'll never discern
who you really are
till you stop believing
who you're told you are

...

never apologize
for refusing to conceal
blunt truths with clever lies

49

notice:
mainstream culture prefers
to condemn rather than forgive
to destroy rather than build
to impose rather than lead
to horde rather than give
to lecture rather than listen
to divide rather than unify
to force rather than guide
to lie rather than edify
to argue rather than agree
to control rather than free
to waste rather than save

so is there really any question
as to why we of modernity
seem to have lost
our way?

...

compromise
only compromises
those compromised
by a pride hypnotized
in the web of cultish lies

50

from fire to light
ignites the soul's delight
upon bonds of temporal bondage
being finally untied

...

no facile desire
could ever hope to match
the sacredness of the match
which sparks our innermost
sacred fire

...

the higher you go
the further you'll feel
the lesser you'll know
the deeper surreal

51

consider:
reality's reality is only so
insomuch as our perceptions
are taken to be objective
but if we could ask say
the bats and the bees
who saw more authentically
both would win their argument
for each has an awareness
of a subjective realness made evident
diversity being but a performance
in the fathomless theater of oneness
yet we'd rather
cleave and blame
destroy and maim
than together enjoy
and celebrate the
grandiose play

shame

52

life is bound
to bring unforeseen rains
but why should that mean
they must ruin our days?

...

as wounds must breathe
in order to wholly heal
so to hearts must forgive
before they may wholly feel

...

if you can master
your appetite and
the foods you consume
likewise can you master
anything you choose

53

notice:
the inauthentic being
is incapable of
authentically
perceiving

…

authentic intelligence
beams in vivid view
upon one eradicating
a falsity and
adopting
a truth

…

discrimination
is to illumination
what ignorance
is to intoxication

54

peel away
what happened before
and be this moment
at once reborn

...

dust away the yesterdays
ashes of past ways
gone tomorrow
reset the day
begin anew
renewed
today

...

our societal systems
are systematically structured
to siphon our souls

but you have asylum
free from clamor and crisis
in the caverns of your mind
where the true Self thrives
amid a glorious silence

55

it's sad to say
but some are so full of hate
that they'll hate you for nothing more
than your unwillingness to hate
what they themselves implore

...

notice:
the same things
that unite us
to bind us
some use
to divide us
and blind us

...

when the world
backs insanity in mass
the sane deploy memes
as red pills fueled with laughs

56

until the heart
is willing to change
mankind shall strain
till the end of days

...

notice:
in many cases
the loudest statement
is pure nonparticipation

...

realize:
the world may come to hate you
but do recall the truth that
the world bows to
none other than
the One who
made you

57

they say
not to sweat
the small stuff
and that it's all small
but with those you love
you'd be remiss to forget
not to treasure it all
for although all is small
with them it's still all
you'll ever get

...

they say
we can always find
something to be thankful for
but notice how many of us
nearly always give thanks
for something other than
the ability to breathe
and our right to be
living free

58

when your sober
transmutes into
your new high
you've realized
there is only
the Most
High

...

consider:
sensory reality
is but an evanescent layer
upon layers and layers of ethereal wallpaper
created by the utmost creative Creator
who decorates as the most decorated Decorator
experienced as consciousness
expressed in nature

...

after the womb is life
before the tomb is breathe
between and beyond them both
is the Self

59

the most fundamental right
is the freedom for us to explore
the depths of our own minds

...

until
we are free
to experiment on
our consciousness as
our conscience deems fit
all critical talks of freedom
are but hypocritical lip service

...

everyone has a few loose screws
but not everyone has determined
exactly which ones they
have loose

so goes a mechanic of the mind
who repairs wear and tears
before breakdowns
breakdown their
mind

60

as the individual journey
is the true destination
so to indivisible oneness
is the true revelation

...

keep striving
for more often than not
accomplishment is contingent upon
the will to keep climbing

...

to face
a daunting unknown
is to enter shadows alone
but never feel obliged
to flee in fear of night
for what is darkness to you
who walks as conscious light?

61

those who deny
the One infinite nature
inevitably end up accepting
the legions of finite imitators

...

the perishable will temp you
the imperishable will enrich you

...

those who aspire the spirit inspire
those who idolize the idols beguile

...

if a picture paints a thousand words
then an idea inhales a million dreams
what do you see?
what will you be?
what will you paint?
what do you dream?

62

will you keep
paradigms designed to keep
the human spirit mentally weak
worshiping the ever corrosive trends
of cancer-culture and cultist groupthink?

...

will you eradicate
your deepest convictions
just to rationalize the atrocities
and acquiesce to fallacious policies
endorsed by statists in political parties?

...

if we've learned one thing
over the last few years
it's that fear controlled
will control the world
in controlling fears

...

the mainstream will have you
love what's fake and hate what's true

63

the elixir
is in the mirror

...

the remedy
is in the tragedy

...

the healing
is in the feeling

...

center your mind
on becoming aligned
with the truths inside
instead of the noise said
outside your head
by which angst is fed

64

a mind full
is no more mindful
than the mindless fool

...

be mindful of the mindlessness
seeking to mine your consciousness
being ever so prevalent in
this age of vast deception
but the veil is now lifting
so all with eyes to see
and ears to hear
may witness
the fullness
of God's
promises

...

conscious
seekers suffer
an illness of inwardness
because they know the pains
of their own former ignorance

65

the Celestial Composer
evermore composes
realities harmonious
to all audiences
who are free to
ignore or
notice

...

music echoes
magnetic motions
manifesting within us
as melodious emotions

...

all are ascribed
an aspiration to awaken
abilities assiduously arising
from awakening's activation

66

the thinker
is above the thought

...

the prover
is between the proof

...

the user
is within the used

...

what we outgrow
we must let go

...

let the past go
and watch thyself grow
is ways once impossible
for you to ever imagine
let alone know

67

facts do not speak
to those who see without vision
and hear but don't listen

...

if facts cause you to rampage
in emotional distress
then perhaps you should
ask yourself why
and reassess

...

facts are only offensive
to those of whom truth shatters
the platitudes of their political agendas

...

when a society
teaches its citizens
not to question anything
but to robotically obey instead
it will unavoidably end up treating
all those who refuse to do so as a threat

68

the highroad
is taken by those
who let their baggage go
so misery's undertow
can't drag them down
into the dark depths
of regret below

...

everything looks better
with a higher perspective

...

stars would be
a shineless blaze
if not for lightless space

...

notice:
when focus
becomes focused
the focal points
become noticed

69

so compelling is
the love innate in light
that its presence compels
the Primordial Light
to conceive
new life

...

life is light
light is love
love is grace
divinely designed
as grace radiates the love
of God's Light within all life

...

life breathes
to the beat of light beams
bountifully beaming between
boundless realities

70

do you remember
when you were fearless?
for even in a crowd you were
impossible to miss

….

fear is only a virtue
to those who fearmonger
in an effort to control you

…

that which disturbs
defensiveness loose
is so often what
we fear to lose

…

action
through non-action
is the wisest reaction
when chaos and passion
are the warring factions

71

what are we
if not reveries of the universe
witnessed through light
rehearsed in verse?

...

what are we
if not a paradox
of paradoxical thoughts
in a mysterious box
left mysteriously
unlocked?

...

what are we
if not an inheritance
of nature's transcendence
via our spiritual awareness?

...

what are we
if not reflections
of our deepest impressions?

72

what are we
if not a miraculous myth
of ancestral consciousness?

...

what are we
if not a single melody
playing automatically on repeat?

...

what are we
if not the chosen offspring
coded by the Master's master key?

...

what are we
if not sentient stardust
immune to injury and rust?

...

what are we
if not atoms aware they're alive?

73

everything we take for granted
will eventually leave us empty handed

...

even the best of things
will become at best mundane
if they're taken to the extreme
and abused in vain

...

there are unique instances
when all an outside opinion will do
is cause you to second guess yourself
and become confused

...

denial and acceptance
are only separated by
a will who elects

74

blessed
are the wounds
whose blemishes blessed you
into becoming the best you

...

glorious
is the journey
which converts suffering into mercy
glorifying spiritual over material glory

...

hallelujah
to the hallowed art
of piecing back the pieces of a broken heart
so love may one day securely restart

75

those who
demand a life for a life
condemn the whole world
to die in suicidal strife

...

notice:
a heart deep in spite
will deeply torment a life
as would a thousand rusted cuts
from a blunt butcher knife

...

those who
in power will
press for immunity
from any fair criticism
are so often infected with
a self-made strain of narcissism
fused with pathological barbarism

76

the hardest things
we have to do
are always the things
we have to do

...

it's so easy to give in and quit
perhaps that's why accomplishment
is a most daunting precipice
to which it's ourselves
with whom we're
up against

...

good things happen
to those who wait
great things happen
to those who create
glorious things happen
to those who pray

77

what's a dark night
to a dark knight?
have you conquered your night
to liberate your inner knight?
have you beheld the abyss
where fear arrives to die?
as even death has its time
to pass beyond time
and where darkness
meets the light
there you'll find
your dark knight
above good and evil
between wrong and right
for when ego
and spirit align
you'll become so
bright in the dark
that even your
shadow shines

...

careful
not to mistake
living a life you hate
simply for comfort's sake

remember:
it's easy to inflate the insignificant
when things are going so magnificent

...

there's nothing worse
than roasting in a sauna
of self-inflicted drama

...

consider:
what we do not heal
becomes hell
what we do not forgive
we relive

...

the pains from true love
ignite certainty's flames

79

bliss is
now*here*
don't you see?
what we perceive
is not an actuality
it's what we believe
which becomes our reality

...

perhaps the
secret ingredient
to happiness rests
in being flexible
and innovative with
what we use for
our ingredients

...

disquietude
promptly concludes
when acceptance
serenades your
moods

80

the reward from the test
is awarded in lessons
only fully apprehended
upon one being
tested

...

when we fail to put forth
the best of our ability
the best we can do
is fail ourselves
completely

...

those who refuse
to ever change their mind
have made up their mind
to mentally die

81

consider:
that if you
surely love someone
sometimes you must
willingly let them go
so perhaps that they
may on their own
come to testify of
share and know
the sure love
you hold

so it is with God
and all creation below

...

sometimes
taking a step back
is the only way to progress
by granting space to apprehend
what our reason once had lacked
and our hearts prior to had missed

82

if today just isn't your day
consider going out of your way
to make another's day today

...

there's much
to complain about
during dreary times
but do notice if you might
the sun's brilliance still beams
despite the transitory storms
in our day to day lives

...

either all lives matter
and oneness is taught
or no lives matter
and nihilism is wrought
anything in-between
is but a prejudice thought
and the prejudiced mind
calls division its god

83

sadness
is just our happiness
flipped on its head
when we least
expect

...

the truth of feeling
doubtlessly depleted
and undoubtedly down
is that it's only you who
can lift yourself upright to
the harbor of higher ground

...

the quickest route to regret
is arguing while you're already upset

....

maybe there's
nothing more you can do
but maybe that's
more than
enough

84

more dreams
have met their demise
before the chance at life
on behalf of bad advice
than failure itself
could ever hope
to devise

...

never abort
your dreams to appease
those who couldn't
begin to fathom
the dreams you've
dreamed

...

your destiny
is only destined
insomuch as your resolution
believes either your own projections
or those reflected from outsider's impressions

85

silence
is infinite
what a twist
fullness in nothingness

...

chaos is to creation
as revelation is to manifestation
what purpose is to predestination

...

may you laugh in the face
of all the absurdities you'll face

...

the absurd
remains absurd
until the Word
of God is felt
and heard

86

those who rant
about capricious privilege
do little other than belittle
by abetting animosity absorbed
in misdirected frustration worn
for it matters not
the size crib one's placed in
nor the body one's soul inherited
for all must play the cards they're dealt
so to craft one's own distinctive meaning
is the authentic privilege of existence felt

...

notice:
one's entire constitution
shall mutate into the animal state
should reason for tribalism be replaced

...

tis greater
to fail whilst
being authentic to oneself
than to conquer the whole world
whilst in the shoes of someone else

87

isn't it so
all are engaged
in a daily personal war
others may never come to know
yet in the face of such unique battles
underneath what appearances may show
recognize all are irrevocably connected
to an ethereal Force of ineffable glow
the Source by whom fortitude flows
and so when it seems the pressures
of your relentless stressors
and aggressors will win
or deep in anguish
you find yourself
about to give in
realize this
that you don't have to bear
your many encumbers all alone
for the Most High's brightest Light
is forever aware and eagerly prepared
to lighten the load and brighten the roads
needed to shepherd your weary soul home

88

why do less
than what you know
you're capable of doing
when what you're capable of
is less about what you know
than it is what you're capable
of doing in spite of the unknown?

...

improvements don't occur
just by uttering the word aspiration
learning doesn't ensue
just by saying the word education
success doesn't arise
just by mouthing the word determination
ergo
that which
we want or need
shall be a vain imagination
till we put forth the effort to
bring about its manifestation

89

how much we come to grow
is dependent on
how much we want to know
and
how much we come to know
is contingent on
how much we want to grow

*so the saying goes
to each their own*

...

even the transmuting cocoon
is doomed to mutate into a tomb
if it's never broken through
and removed by the being
in bloom

*so it is should one reject
the spiritual metamorphosis
their soul seeks to direct*

90

why do you
always second guess
the one you've always
known best?

...

there are many puzzles
you'll deem worth pursuing
their many pieces for solving
but see the greatest of these
is as a puzzle of undoing
the pieces from the one
who first deems
a pursuit worth
starting

so it is when
one has taken
their mind apart
and put back again
to see the picture of how
their individual puzzle
pictures the world
and themselves

91

before any benefits
of believing in a belief
can be verily reaped
one must first be seeded
with a validating belief
that the belief to be believed
is beneficial to believe

...

those who realize
their beliefs were bequeathed
sooner or later must ask themselves
if they actually believe what they preach
or have been operating involuntarily
in a most automated routine
thoughtlessly accepting
and following in
the footprints
of other's
beliefs

such is the first stage to blossoming anew
the evaluation of the beliefs we cling to

92

be open
to being open
and new doors will open
that you didn't know
you didn't know
could be opened
let alone openly known
even free for you
to freely roam

...

freely arise
from beneath
the secular sheath
in which the pure you hides
to realize the impotence in any attempt
at diminishing thy innate celestial shine

...

look between
to make the unseen seen

93

notice:
drawing a line
with regards to
someone close to you
can be quite easier
said than done
for with every line
drawn and crossed
you'll be drawn closer
to being quite done
with the one who
continues to
pay no mind
to your line

*so it is when life makes us choose
to let go or hold onto those who deliberately
and repeatedly ignore our personal rules*

...

you should always know
what's important to
those who are
important
to you

94

why if humanity is so connected
do so many humans feel
so utterly rejected?

...

why in cities of plenty
do plenty of hearts feel
so heartlessly empty?

...

why with ample opportunity
do countless choose to live
in abject lethargy?

perhaps because
a plague of fakeness
plagues our generation
from fake faces to fake news
to fake friends and fake foods
and the only way to end this plague
is to be so real that everything you do and say
is a rebellion against everything that's fake

95

the key to God
seems concealed until
one discovers that
never was there
ever any lock
holding us
back

...

self-restraint
is a self-aware saint

...

sacrifice
is the seed of life

...

duty
is the valor of deity

96

too often in religion
do the religious blindly listen
to the authorities of their religions

...

too little in spiritually
do the spiritual actually practice
the messages from the messengers

...

just right
will both sides
before they capsize
together realize
they're passengers
on the same boat
in a single seat
sailing seas
of affirmations
sharing salutations
as intimate hymns
to Divinity disguised
within the multiplicity
of life

97

the only thing
we have to lose
is that which
we fear to lose

...

your voyage
may not always fare
neatly or straight paced
but so long as
you're voyaging forward
trust that you're well on
your way

...

consider:
don't be so eager
to write everything off
before it even has the chance
to be written at all

98

as the
act of giving
is itself the gift
so to selfless love
so selfishly devoted
is as adoration gifted
for mutual betterment

...

service to each other
selflessness towards another
God's love undercover

...

love is the seed that supersedes
all logic and thinking
forever sprouting
lovely scenes
of God
made
seen

99

the core proof
despotic censoring proves
is that such despot censors
are always petrified by
vocal voices of truth
as seen in the
rabid censorship
they deliberately use
and with impunity abuse
the rights of all to voice
their uncensored views

...

political correctness
is truth's death sentence

...

if you're powerless to control it
why give it the power to control you?

100

it seems to me that the key resides
not in adopting a single philosophy or system
but in embracing endless possibilities
alive inside the mental kingdom
which embellish existence and
bestow purpose upon life's
intimately infinite
unified rhythm

…

find the middle
or find yourself
wandering hazardous dunes
behold the balance
or behold yourself
inhaling fanatical fumes
hear the subtlety
or hear yourself
regurgitating partisan views

…

as nuance dies
extremism will rise

101

the strings we used to obey
when fast asleep our spirits laid
have no power over us today
now that we're finally awake

...

the notions
'live and let be' or
'live according to what pleases me'
are akin to the paradigms of
'equality of opportunity'
and *'equality of outcome'*
the former are as an offspring of liberty
the latter are but an accomplice in tyranny

...

dependence on the state
resurrects the wickedness of slavery
only in monetary weights

102

the karma
of today's youth
is to constantly roam
between falsity and truth

…

wonder
is wonderfully witnessed
is all the wonderful hearts
of our wondrous children
who love with the love
of godly vision

…

perhaps the secret
behind the wisdom in aging
is the wisdom in preventing
the child within us from fading

103

o' thou of youthfulness!
amid all the decisive decisions
of thy youth demand be made
few are more demanding than
deciding the friendships
as companions to
accompany you
throughout
your days
also those
you must
abandon
and afar
away
stay

...

consider:
that a friendship
you may wish to see flourish
will be impossible to cultivate
if all your desired friend does
is toil your soil in bad faith
and water your buds with
passive-aggressive hate

104

cracks
don't break us
nor define us
rather they
reshape us
realign us
redesign us
and remind us
how far past
we've passed the past
refusing along the way
to shatter or collapse

…

notice:
a diamond
will only form
when deep within
under pressure and heat
a rock is reborn

so it is with
the elemental you
a transformation thanks to
the many forces you've ensued

105

animosity
is effortless
it's forgiveness
that's arduous

...

arrogance
is common
it's modesty
that's foreign

...

angst
is mortal
it's patience
that's providence

...

death should be
the least of our worries
for what is more worrisome
would be a need for returning
having to start again relearning

106

faith is devoted
to faithfully devoting
faithfulness in devotion
by all the faithful awoken

...

before we could speak
we laughed
before we could run
we danced
before we could doubt
we believed
before we could worry
we dreamed

...

there's a majesty in meekness
no amount of money could mimic
nor force of might manage to diminish

107

the chains of hate
will chain you to pain
and imprison you in rage
while the key that is grace
gracefully opens every cage

...

to permit
the continuation
of a known cancer
is to slice your throat
with your own dagger

...

you can aimlessly obsess
over the cards others were dealt
or work to maximize the hand
you've been endowed with yourself

108

you are
neither the shadow
in your substance
nor the substance
in your shadow
but an echo
of the echoes
from the micro
to the vaster
from the novice
to the master
to the actor
and director
both the first
and last chapter
as the former
and the after
in the moment
and future after

…

have you
ever wondered
how many truly know
they're a *god* in human clothes?

109

if less is more
than more or less
less is better but
more of less is best

...

the best plan of action
is often one that's best
at doing more and
talking less

...

sometimes
you must go
with what you know
you know
even if you don't know
why or how you know
what you know
you know

110

you
are more priceless
than the rarest jewel
for you have discovered
that the rarest jewel
is the priceless
you

...

a flower doesn't instantly bloom
but when it's due it's instantly beautiful

*so it is
with the cultivation
of the true you*

...

sometimes
just waking up
to continue the day again
is heroic enough to be considered
superhuman

111

the child doesn't realize
what it means to be a parent
until said child
is themselves a parent
so it's not that odd
why we're unable to comprehend
that we are a god
until we encounter and witness
our real nature as the Atman
for the Atman is Brahman

so it is said that
Thou Art That

…

love past
the reasoning mind
is a paradigm transcending
reason and time

112

when the ego
is made a servant
and the mind stills observant
the soul exercises discernment
galvanizing light to beam emergent
within us brighter than the firmament

...

even though clouds may cover the sky
we know that behind the sun still abides
so it is with the ego to whom we find
clouding the true Self who inerrantly shines

...

baptized
in brightness
all souls gravitate
towards their likeness

113

the seer is both
the seeing and the seen

...

the dreamer is both
the dreaming and the dreamed

...

the prover is both
the proving and the proven

...

friend:
keep radiating
your effulgent light
for you may just end up
inadvertently healing a life

114

if the fuel
that fuels you
is not your true self
then soon you'll be consumed
in the fumes of everyone else

...

if you allow others
to determine who you are
then you're determined to watch
your individuality sail away afar

...

it's hopeless
to try to please
those who are pleased
to hope for and take pleasure in
your failings

115

the proof of faith
is in the faithful who live it
the truth of the lover
is in the love that's given
the strength of the spirit
is in the spiritually resilient
the reality of existence
is in the real existing in us

...

when tear ducts swell
moist cheeks glisten
fresh wounds rage
pains wail vivid
no greater moment
for that minute lives
than to call upon God
with thy quivering lips

...

you'll never feel more free
than when the real you
is freed from
your body

116

notice:
from the vantage
of the highest peak
we could conceivably see
the shrub and tree
bird and beast
canyon and ravine
ocean and sea
seem to blend into a single scene
losing all distinctions of differences perceived
akin to wakefulness compared to the dream
and so it is with the highest ideal
that being the oneness of all reality
varying *not* in kind
only by degree

…

new pastures
with fresh greens
may not be so novel
nor healthy and green
than from the garden in which
you currently cultivate and eat

117

observe:
once the snake
is mindfully exposed
by discernment known
from realization's glow
to be but a mere rope
superstition's cloak
and ignorance's robe
are permanently unclothed

...

when appetites
are kept nearest to emptiness
it's as if the spirit is naked
in immediate awareness

...

when appetites
are kept nearest to neediness
it's as if the spirit is cloaked
in remote appearances

118

see
the ethereal as spontaneous tears shed
and sacredness in newborn fingers
embrace the present as an endless end
waves of intention unfolding fate
possibilities inspire in whispers
see
harmony throughout pupils of inner sight
and truth in both spirit and shell
one breath guiding souls in flight
celestial nourishment flowing
from a bountiful well
see
faith blossom in sinners turned sages
and empathy sing in silent intuition
realized minds thrive in all ages
peace in spite of any cultural
or political imposition
see
beyond hollow material opulence
and paint deeds of wisdom and love
there is *no* religion higher
than consciousness purified
one nature
as above so below
as below so above

119

only you
can save you
for it is your choice
to disbelieve or believe
in the beliefs that make it
false or true

...

consider:
that each of us live
as idiosyncratic mirrors
mirroring unique grades
of an infinite Lamp effulgent
despite the fabricated haze
from our self-imposed shades

...

it's futile
to foster your truth
if you obsessively fixate
over what others think of you

120

notice:
we can agree to disagree
or not disagree and agree
but either way
unless we preserve
our freedom of speech
soon neither of us will
have the ability to say
anything

...

if ideologues and demagogues
are freely allowed to police our speech
soon they'll be free to prosecute us
for nothing more than how we think

...

praise be to the just who
are unjustly forced to suffer
for nothing other than the integrity
of what their conscience freely utters

121

babe to teen and adult to elder
form transforms but the soul is sheltered
awareness beneath as the utmost treasure
and although the body eventually surrenders
the spirit carries on from forever to forever

...

at times
only tuning out
will tune you in
only turning off
will turn you on
whereupon
your awareness becomes
as warmth from a most
invigorating sun

...

doing nothing
everything done
desiring nothing
everything won

122

the One self
breathes life into breath
speaking forth from the breathing
as Itself willed to flesh

...

the ground of all being
is found in all beings
grounded in consciousness
whereby
the conscious being
is both the purpose and meaning
for everything

...

inner awareness
consciously awake
inner numbness
unconsciously fake

123

we won't always get what we want
and we won't always want what we get
yet we can always strive to be content
costing amid the waves of acceptance

...

there are moments when
changes are only welcomed
following an unwelcoming moment

...

the deeds we humans do
disclose more truth
than our tongues
could ever hope
to prove

...

be vigilant so as
not to hastily pursue
practices and habits which
will slowly decompose you

124

why do you care
if others care
or don't
care?

...

why look to raise the bar
when you can be
the bar?

...

why
even begin to
follow the crowd
when it's so crowded that
most can barely move around
but by the time they realize
they've followed enough
and finally want out
they'll have to on
their own find
their way
out

you're the Most High individualized
in a sheath individually designed
to harbor your individual shine
but once this is realized
you'll never fit back inside
no returns to the womb
yet born again still
only this time
of light

...

the urge to create
cannot be replaced
it can only be repressed
with diversions that waste
the initial creative urge
all potential creators face

why wait to create?
you do it before
you realize
it's too
late

a most
demoralizing choice
your opinions can choose
is to assume the dim notions
your darkness says of you are true

…

inspiration is hydration
encouragement is nourishment
positivity is durability
know very few will lift you up
many more will drag you down
while some will push you left
others will shove you right
yet you have your own wings
you need only take flight

…

a most courageous act
you can courageously do
is have the courage
to speak up for
none other
than you

127

notice:
at the foot
of the mountain
plant we a feet
before a precipice each
may choose to hike
up slopes unique
following many
of diverse trails
and streams
till
at the summit we
meet and greet
discovering the truth
that God is
not just the peak
but the entire vista
endured and seen
from you and me
to everything
in between

moderation
is the master key
to a most masterful
inner peace

…

the aptness
to alter an opinion
is the power to release oneself
from any and all ideological prisons

…

peace prevails
when inner acceptance
becomes externally reflected

129

outer ease
cannot increase
till inner resentment
is wholeheartedly released

...

sadness
comes and goes
like a season
at times it's random
other times for a reason
but one may suppose the goal
is not to stumble uneven
after all
despite the most savage of winds
still stands the lighthouse beacon

...

routine will
kill your ambition
if allowed to become
a stagnating addiction

130

consider:
all freedoms owe a debt
to the freedom to object
in speech and conscience
or peaceful protest
for without it we
could do little save
conform and submit

...

remember:
your freedom
does not end when
another's fear begins

...

times were easier
when you were asleep
for it's the easy times
which easily make one weak

*but now you're awake and
although the struggles are deep
from amid the abyss of the pains
arose someone anything buy weak*

131

our path
only goes as far as
we're willing to pave
our own roads

...

those opposed
to their own cerebral changes
are as books repeating
their opening pages

...

as pacifying water
that gracefully bends
so to the honest seeker
whose opinion amends

132

reality is a hive mind
electrically entwined
consciously aligned
perceptually refined
designed

…

notice:
blessings seem ripple in enigmatic disguise
while afflictions roar in conspicuous skies
but the response and recognition of both
has one but one common denominator
thy own eyes

…

the brightest spirits
immersed in righteousness
shined the utmost when
persevering under
suffering eyelids

133

last year you said last month
last month you said last week
last week you said yesterday
yesterday you said today
today you said tomorrow
tomorrow you'll say _____

...

realize:
one can earn
lost money back
upon having been
spent on memories
but one can never
earn back memories
upon having been
lost to money
unspent

spirituality is a seed
which leads to roots of buried truths
and fruits of inner awakenings

…

spirituality is a journey
of manifesting the best version
of your highest person

…

spirituality is as a perennial art
in the embark to integrate
the villainous shadow
with the virtue of
the noble
heart

135

faith burns away the veil
while incinerating fear
kindling a certitude
of truth aflame
seen for the
first time
crystal
clear

...

love welcomed in
welcomes in forgiveness
welcomingly forgiving
the once unforgiven

...

faith is love visualized
love is faith internalized
spirit and will galvanized
body and mind synchronized

an excuse
for an incompetence
is the hypocrite's last line
of desperate defense

...

irony is satisfyingly ironic
especially when karma
teaches frauds how it feels
to be defrauded

...

karma is only a bitch
to the hypocrite who's full of shit

137

what actual truth
we may actually surmise
can only be found in
a flow below
the ego's
eyes

...

the mind in command
of what its ego compels
is where paradise dwells

...

place the ego in constraints
to open the ethereal planes

...

the ego exists in external excess
the spirit subsists in self subsistence

138

perhaps
the only error
in all of creation
is the thinking that errors
could have ever been created

...

consider:
a stumble we
easily stumble across
is the thinking that a path
couldn't have been crossed

...

it seems
the trouble is not
in what trouble gives
but in finding someone
to share our troubles with

139

spiritual revolutions
begin by awakening love
political revolutions
being by shedding blood
will we have piece
or be in pieces?
to each their own
but each must own
the reality they
transmit

...

betwixt breath and silence
resides love and violence
as forms of experience
in liveliness

...

the ones who clamor to erase history
are fated to relive its every misery

140

'new normal'
is just a euphemistic phrase
for humanity's inalienable liberties
vanishing in insidiously novel ways

...

quarantine isolates the ill
tyranny imprisons the well

...

there's nothing normal
about accepting an abnormal normal
in the hope of getting back to *'normal'*

...

quarantine
causes the cogs to be conscious
of the obscene machine underneath

141

love will crush *and* caress you

...

truth will free *and* possess you

...

hope will bless *and* depress you

...

notice::
there are times
when by seeking to
wait for the right time
you'll never be satisfied
and only waste your time

...

if misery
loves company
then euphoria
loves privacy

142

what you think and utter
will mold your reality
one way or another

...

words are swords
which slice and shape
form and create reality
with spellings as spells
spoken and tossed down
our personal wishing wells

...

just as
the flute is not the player
but the played
the body is not the user
but the used
for what's viewed
is not what's true
but rather the view
of tools in use
by the ultimate truth
the imperishable you

143

a pearl
only dwells
in *very few* shells

...

excuses planted
sprout trees which wither
procrastination's soil
spoils roses like winter

...

sometimes
we tell ourselves
unconvincing lies
like the simple times
won't be remembered
as the best days of
our lives

144

the danger is taught
in systems that rid us the need
for critical thought

...

when reason is muzzled
and seldom sought
discourse sours
and rots

...

knowledge is debased
when indoctrination
as education is
embraced

145

stop giving
what stresses you out
all the time of your day
and feel your stress
fade away

...

the sands of stress
disintegrate with every breath

...

the worst of stress
is caused by nothing less
than a mind in a state of unrest

146

save me a spot
right next to you at your mosque

...

save me a seat
at your church in the pews beside you

...

let's meet at the mental temple
beyond angels and devils

...

between fire and ice
there is light
between good and evil
there is sight
between peace and war
there is might
between fact and fiction
there is right
between heaven and hell
there is life

147

'I am second'
some prefer to say
but it is this illusion
of secondness via separateness
which leads minds and spirits astray

...

perhaps
it is we who bend
rather than the spoon
for is it not we who are one
rather than two?
one sun with many views
one secret but many clues
one *'I'* and many *'yous'*

...

the specter of separation
is the utmost chimerical
of materialist imaginations

148

consider:
there will be
some you meet
who find it easy
enjoyable even
to backbite about you
when you're not in view
with apparently nothing
more beneficial to do
than try to belittle you
but give this little care
pay it none of your time
for in the shortest time
it'll have left your mind
but for the one who
acted ill towards you
until they come change
the flaws in their ways
they'll wonder why
they always feel
hollow inside
to no reply
except a
silent
cry

149

the present of awareness
is the awareness of the present

...

the purpose of existence
is to be purposefully existing

...

the closer
you perceive
the more reality
becomes illusionary

...

illusions
are illusionary
to the illuminated

150

do not be afraid
of chiseling away
old blocks of rock
that others carved
for you in the name
of sculpting you in stone
like a statue all the same
as everyone else who
was carved before they
even had the chance to say
if they wanted to be carved
and set in stone in the first place

...

consider:
there's a method to our madness
and a madness to our methods
the only difference is
some are self-improving
others self-antagonists
and it's up to each
to discover the madness
they either profess or reject
to then correct or perfect

151

there is
that which is *right*
that which is *right for now*
and that which is *right now*
the differences being
quite profound

…

to recognize what's right
one must risk being wrong

…

to distinguish what's fact
one must extinguish what's false

152

you either
grow or erode

...

you either
live out your dreams
or continue to sleep

...

you either
free yourself via spirituality
or remain caged in physicality

153

perhaps the problem
is our perception of the problem

...

each perception
offers unique suggestions
to both answers and questions

...

if you must judge
do so not strictly on behalf
of what one claims to know
but do so based off
the questions they asked
which helped them arrive at
their presumed knowledge's home

154

why do
you desire
conformity
to blend
when you
were crafted
unique
to become?

...

why does
your gaze
fixate on
the ground
when your
eyes were
forged in
the firmament?

155

there's meaning in the mystery
and mystery in the meaning

...

the mystery of life
is life's mystery
made alive

...

life's a metaphor
for something more
to which all the cognizant shall
for themselves define and explore

...

consider:
if there were already
a ready-made answer for everything
nothing would mean absolutely anything

156

failings are teachers
ambitions are leaders

...

light reveals breadth
shadow reveals depth

...

duties reveal mentality
pleasures reveal personality

157

knock
and be let in
how you're received
is in accordance with
how you've lived

...

don't forget:
it's the spiritually dead
who will attempt
to cannibalize
your spirit
remiss of
regret

...

somewhere
through meadows
of sun-kissed flowers
and miles of old asphalt
at the feet of metal cages
resides a valley of hope for
our homesick human race

158

the fundamental goal
is mastery over the ego
to feel the Master who is
the Fundamental Soul

…

a conquered ego
is the utmost treasure
as it permits one
to see through
all biases
and see beyond
all pleasures

159

only the truthful
can see the truth
in full

...

what knowledge
could be more truthful
than that which makes
the spirit youthful?

...

those that
are spiritual
are spirit full

160

to do what
you've never done
you must think how
you've never thought

...

if you wish
to bask in new sensations
you must first unmask
your old limitations

...

a new
idea entertained
doesn't have to be accepted
in order to simply be respected

161

amongst the visible rivers
of experience and observation
consists an invisible ocean
of intuition and imagination

...

is the world
truly what you see
or is what's perceived
but the inner waves
of an ethereal sea?

...

those forces whom
seem greatly opposed
are as balancing petals
complimenting a most
picturesque rose

162

'bless God'
and *'bless you'*
is but one prayer
under one roof

...

you're
a star child
carefully styled
intentionally incarnate
for a short while

...

perhaps the divine
is as a mansion or inn
ever spacious inside with
a myriad of unique ways in

163

have you ever
gazed within so deep
you sensed all sensations
evaporate obsolete
into an ecstasy
beyond every
expression?

*so it is
in those who emerge
from their meditations with God
having all hindrances been purged*

…

let go
are they
whom let go
how to not
not let go

164

if you don't believe
in all that you are and
may become yet still
who else will?

...

self-faith
cannot be taken
let alone replace by
anyone besides the self
in whom said faith resides

...

until you
consciously know thyself
the world will attempt to
subconsciously convince you
that you're someone else

165

notice:
the loudest voices
barking so proudly
are rarely versed in
the elegant subtitles
which always magnify
all listeners so lovingly

...

consider:
the baggage
you've carried
like a carry on
has carried on
for far too long
and that it's time
for you to let it go
and journey on

166

don't take the bait
to be divided by race

...

those who race
to only see race
see naught but their
own prejudice staring
themselves in the face

...

consider:
you don't have enemies
only mirrors of your psyche
showing you what you would be
if you surrendered to
your own shadow's
tyranny

167

how did you decide
to believe what you decided?
traditions passed down
like David and Goliath?
convictions popularized
by demagogues and idols?
advertised paradigms
paid for by your honor?
think it over mindful
for belief is like air
absorbed
filtered
exhaled
vital

...

how many
in this age and day
pride themselves on
how thoroughly they obey
giddily sacrificing their reason
gladly squandering their energy
merely to reinforce regulations
their rulers haphazardly relay

168

wish not
to be easily and
needlessly offended
for as hopes swell
selves will satisfy
the wishes ever so
easy to fulfill

...

notice:
how often
some are offended
simply by a simple opinion

...

the less that offends you
the more who will befriend you

169

the body decays
but the soul transforms

...

death
is the awareness
that makes life precious

...

the *only* deaths
that permanently die
are those that perish
within us while
we're still
alive

...

death is not the end
but the first sentence
of a new chapter to begin

we are angels
wrong or right
face or flight
measured by our angles
dark or light
rise or plight

...

that which was
was always done
but that which is
is always begun

...

as above
so below
get what you put in
reap what you sow

171

these are the days
in which the dozing hath blamed
their every pain on an unjust fate
but what is fate to those awake
if not a vast horizon with ample terrain
to break old habits and build new ways

...

fate
in its own fateful way
makes us pay attention
to every connection
that fatefully comes
our direction

...

your fate
dyes the hue
of the character you
fatefully morph yourself into
with every passing thing you choose

172

to know your worth
is to be worth your knowledge

...

to master your will
is to be willfully masterful

...

the power of balance
is the balance of power

...

true power
is the power
to truly will
your will
power

173

'everything is fine'
said the lie
to the reflection
gazing back into
a past not yet
left behind

...

to restore your mind
is to recover your life
to recover your life
is redemption
realized

so it is when
God given we
let the past go
to begin again

how can you be open
to what a new love might bring
if you're still lost in the heart strings
of a past fling?

...

heart strings strangle
when love becomes tangled

...

true love
will truly arise
when expectations
aren't desperate
to find

175

one never feels
more mindful than
the moments when
they allow themselves
to feel more and mind less

*like listening in
to the child within
and believing again
in the magic of love
and the blessedness
of innocence*

...

imagine if we saw each other
with the pupils of our inner child?

...

every life is
a gift from above
may each kindle
a new childhood
to reunite with
simple loves

176

nature is deemed natural
and this appease most
but what is natural or nature itself
if not a precise code clothed
by a supernatural host
the One as one
only appearing manifold?
yet the supernatural is ridiculed
by some with a skeptical groan
but before they bemoan
they must know the super *is* natural
simply before discovery makes
its natural nature known

...

engineer or magician
scientist or shaman
the differences are but letters
and capricious definitions
for all seek to know God by
mimicking the Lord's dearest of devices
as experience and invention
creativity and intuition
are but games to
the Most High
Sovereign

177

that which transfixes
your innermost attention
is as a compass which ushers
you towards your future direction
and the future you's inception

...

we must not think
we must believe
everything we
think

...

see that more often than not
we're wrong about what
we initially thought

...

when the mind is watched
and thought is not sought
ego reduces to naught
freeing the true Self
to be met on
the spot

178

all voids emerge
from futile attempts
to repudiate one's essence
by replacing one's Creator

...

once
you see the void
and it sees you back
there's no way to forget it
let alone backtrack

...

the soul
becomes an open book
for those who know
in which plants
to look

...

educate to liberate
meditate to levitate
activate to venerate
participate to demonstrate

179

consider:
you've shed bodies like
skins and scales as assorted attire
time after time again they expire
as such
thy newly pressed
current body suit
will eventually follow suit
and though novel
appearing divergent
than the last outfit
the true soul of you
is no different
nor has it ever been
out of style
as your soul is
the tailor and the buyer
incarnated for a short while
from the Lord of all oneness
the *only* Supplier

180

the preeminent realization
is as a spiritual transmutation
found in personal experience
being intimately cognizant
to which one's consciousness
comes to the conclusive conclusion
that their innermost being
is as a transcendent infusion
only shrouded in provisional illusions

...

self-realization
is a metamorphosis
of personal maturation

...

quarantine the ego
for the spirit to fly free

181

notice:
at times
we waste more time
wishing for more time
than we do harnessing
the time allotted to us
to make the most of
our timely lives

...

drink every moment in
for in a moment it will be gone
never to come again

...

have you ever felt flowers pulse in bloom?
have you ever heard light as a silent tune?
have you ever seen a tree as it sees you?
have you ever died inside but rose anew?
a part two
a third eye
have you?

182

realize:
for many these days
the most threatening thing
you can peacefully do
is for yourself think
with the brain
God gave
you

...

thought crime is the latest offense
made criminal by those most thoughtless
who think not for themselves
but rather by the sinister spells
their unconscious programming compels

...

those whose identity
is but an opposite position
only to be in opposition
to a suspected enemy
go about their days
in legion with
infamy

183

the more you
obey the mob
just to fit in neatly
the sooner you'll be
a stranger to yourself completely

...

violent mobs become more brazen
when their audacity is provided
political validation

...

when mob rule
dictates public consciousness
the public will have conceded to
the mobs lawlessness

...

the most radical position
the reasonable can take
is that of indifference
to the radical demands
unreasonable mobs make

184

why focus
on all your flaws
despite all your blessings
from God?

...

o' soul so conflicted
in soulless apparitions!
why choose ye shunneth all
the beauteous blessings thou
hast been bountifully given?

...

o' thou of watchfulness!
be ye ever so watchful
to put thine watch away
and notice how full time
feels when you're fully
watching the moment
and allowing time
to slip away

185

as rage
dominates
the front pages
sages of all races and ages
shall simply choose to disengage with it

…

to say silence is violence
is to say loudness is peace
both notions being equally
absurd and caprice

…

cultivate your brain
not your rage

186

self-reliance
is the only reliable shield
against tyrants whom desire
all powers to wield

...

inequality is less an evil
than is state dependence
championed widespread
and mandated legal

...

vigilant are those citizens
disciplined in perennial principles
defending the liberty of all individuals

...

the radiance
behind liberty's glow
is the freedom to make
mistakes along the way we go

187

love
shall continue to perplex
those who ignore the sages
and signs

...

the pacifist walks
in ascending twilight
past victims and fighters alike

...

Love is
loves are not
Love is formless
loves are a forgery
Love is a process
loves are shortcuts
Love is a pledge
loves are a debt
Love is sacrifice
loves are a vice

188

love is
the formless Lord
made visible into
the world of form

...

love lies in wait
for lovers to follow
the lovely whisperings of fate

...

love that's never known pain
is a romance ill-equipped to sustain

...

love is the phosphorescence
of Christ's conscious essence

189

there's no law
the state won't attempt
to completely circumvent
if the citizenry give in
by giving their consent

...

should a state
answer to itself alone
any action it performs
becomes lawfully condoned

...

the state
will have succeeded
in owning its citizens
when natural rights are viewed as
charitable gifts given

...

stand up for your rights
or you'll be force to sit down
by the force of another's might

190

it's not about
privilege withheld or given
but instead the intensity
of one's will and vision

...

wit
fueled with grit
will get you further
than talent absorbed
in vainglorious arrogance

...

if you don't
know where to begin
start by looking within

...

aspiration to
veneration to
imitation to
illustration to
realization to
identification *with*

191

make no mistake
in a society of deceit
mass producing sheep
the most monumental feat
is maturing into a being unique

...

groupthink mentality
surrenders autonomy and individuality
for dependency and conformity

...

those held to be individual enigmas
will inevitably be judged most unfairly
by the masses superficial stigmas

...

none opens
the inward eye
more thoroughly than
the outward lie

192

consider:
to be called abnormal
by a mainstream culture
obsessed with hedonistic nonsense
corruptible objects and the normalization
of vicarious existence through digital screens
streaming hollow sentiments inundated in
vapid opinions as contrived convictions
from marionette popular figures
and narcissistic grifters
is its own poetic
aesthetic

…

notice:
oft tis only
the nightmare
fated befit for
waking each of us up
by suddenly yanking back
our curtains of illusions
from the abyss whence
no turning back exists

193

verily
thy mystic Word
o' Mystical Lord
teacheth
"I am a part of thee
though I appear apart from thee
for I am the part of thee
etched with the remembrance
of Our inseparable unity"

…

the Lord of Lords
is the door of doors
to worlds upon worlds
for explorers to explore

…

in the
midst of
manifold maya
resonates samsara
and hymns to nirvana
in interlacing webs of karma

194

have you had
the random thought
that thoughts were
neither random
nor yours
to start?

...

have you considered the idea
that everything began as an idea?

...

perhaps all we see
are just scenes out of earth's dreams?

...

what's the chance
reality is ever really left up to chance?

195

be the best you
but know only you'll know
which you is false from true

...

some doors
cannot be noticed
and dare not breached
until walls within us
are breached

...

consider:
that every face
is as the Image of God
begotten in physical space

...

the clay doesn't alter
it's only recycled and remade
into a new altar

196

if your body is your temple
how then are you maintaining?
if your tongue is your scripture
what then are you preaching?
if your deeds are your prophet
how then are you leading?
if your life is as your faith
what then are you teaching?

...

before you act
make the pact that
you will not be attached
to the results your act extracts

*so it is in the minds
of those who choose to do
right purely for the fact
what's right is right to do*

...

if you do because it is true
consequences of the deed done
will be less of a consequence to you

197

consciousness is a single being
disguised as all conscious beings

...

your individual life is the journey
of universal consciousness experiencing the universe
with every page turn of your personal story

...

between physicality and spirituality
is consciousness unmasking reality

...

the living wise
will have learned from life
that the enterprise of living
is as a lesson which provides
one the wisdom in letting go
so in peace go they may
at their appointed day
peacefully accept
their body's will
to naturally
die

198

when silent
one hears all sounds
when still
one feels all motions
when empty
one gains all fullness
when light
one sees all angles
when free
one owns all meanings
when present
one molds all futures
when existing
one becomes all purposes

*discern for yourself
by transcending maya
and awakening thy
inner messiah*

…

die to self
resurrect to spirit
unitive knowledge
personally witnessed
fulfillment in an instant

199

before the millionth
thousandth or hundredth step
of a quest has progressed
the first footprint
must firmly be
pressed

...

often
the question is not
'who told us we could'
but rather
'who told us we couldn't?'

...

truth has no rivals
only deceivers
deniers and
disciples

200

notice:
the beauty of beauty
that it ebbs and flows in rapturous ironies
a poetically personal subjective ambiguity
while auspiciously igniting curiosity's fixations
by arousing vastly vivid aesthetic revelations
experienced explicitly akin to mystical sensations
intoxicating innovations originating organically
all on behalf of beauty animating so beautifully

…

ethereal beauty
boundlessly unborn
manifests as awareness
in the midst of consciousness
allowing spirit to behold the beauty
permeating and animating all forms

201

within the mirror that you view
dwells a messiah alive in you

...

believe there resides
in everyone as light
an Avatar who shines
that anyone can find
and witness the sublime
powers of love and faith
over the mind

...

encased
in everyone
is an energy
imperishable
from element
to embryo
to eternity

202

beyond and betwixt the static
the signal signals streams pneumatic

…

the spirit
saturated in materialism
knowns not of its spiritual wisdom

…

let the spirit awaken
to its spiritual foundation

…

sorrow is
a gateway
to solidarity

203

before growth
comes pain from breaks
for it is the breaks who initiate
the most growth to take place

...

growth is hopeless
unless
you unclothe the personas
which obstruct your
awareness

...

we can never
redo a first impression
but we can always relearn
a lasting lesson

204

imagine what you'd find
by opening your mind

...

take the time
to make peace
with your mind

...

minds over matter
minds matter

...

the unimaginable
exists only to the extent
that one hasn't
imagined it
yet

205

some burn old beliefs
others burn through bills
some burn old bridges
others burn through thrills
for where
there's a will
there's a way
so long as doubt
melts away
after all
what is the will
if not a scale to weigh
all the choices we face
and the prices we pay
to succeed or succumb
thrive or decay

...

change
never stops changing
only evolving and
rearranging

stowed within *'heart'*
is the word *'ear'*
perhaps then
the secret at our
innermost core
radiating eternal love
harnessed within then
to be transmitted
all around us
is simply the conscious
effort made to hear
and listen more
for the frequencies
and vital energies
our hearts
beat for

..

if you're
unwilling to grow
you'll never start
but if you're
determined to grow
you'll never stop

207

the only war
love has known
are the wars our own hands
have sewn

...

sometimes
when we want
what we can't have
we want that which we
can't bring ourselves to take
at least until we refrain
from misleading ourselves
in lies passing others the blame
for us lacking our longing's aim
simply because we've been living
in bad faith

208

isn't it so
that at times
this life feels like
a dream within a dream?
especially when all of a sudden
against our will we perceive
the Perceiver underneath
or synchronicities woven deep
in fractals that never cease
causing déjà vu to creep
around our thoughts as we sleep
but perhaps the real meaning
behind this dreaming dream
is that life is not a riddle
to be unraveled ever swiftly
but an experience to be experienced
and not taken so seriously

...

experience cannot be taught
anymore than love can be bought

209

"we didn't ask to exist
not to see
nor to feel
nor to live
nor to breathe"

said the weed to the tree

"indeed
we didn't choose to be"

replied the tree

"but nature chose you and me
out of all possible plants and greens
to be the seeds who sprout their leaves
so if nothing more
we know one thing our existence means
and that is we're blessed beyond belief"

the weed pondered
over the words
from the tree

"I see what you mean"

said the weed

210

"what have you learned?"

asked identity

*"that superficial labels
isolate us in tribalistic factions
based on facile qualities
which manipulators exploit
by manipulating conversations
with contentious suggestions
pushing heinous policies"*

identity gasped

*"you're a bigot
a racist
a nazi!"*

you rolled your eyes

*"i expected nothing less
from your identitarian ideology
so mechanically and shamelessly professed"*

211

"what have you learned?"

asked reflection

*"that it requires far more energy
lamenting the past than adopting acceptance
and pursuing self-betterment"*

you professed

*"why then have you harkened to the many
false prophets of victimhood and regret?"*

reflection asked

"perhaps it's time to let go instead…"

you reasoned

212

"give the people

synthetic food
ample sport
fake news
addictive meds
empty sex
cheap thrills
strong drink
and watch them
never raise
a concern
nor think
to ever
think

said every despot
with a despotic wink

"what have you learned?"

asked heartbreak

*"that pain from love
conceives a nurturing place
where character may renovate
and learn from mistakes"*

you said

*"become the positive change you
desire your partners to reciprocate"*

heartbreak expressed

214

"what have you learned?"

asked success

"that before I strove
to achieve my dreams
it never occurred to me
the cost of my indolence
would be so steep"

you stated

success agreed

...

"what have you learned?"

asked time

"that there is no storm
detachment cannot weather"

you replied

215

"poor flowers"

said the daughter in dismay

"they've died and passed away"

her father smiled

*"it's true
so it would seem"*

he said kneeling down
beside her by the stream

*"but often life shows us
things aren't often as they seem
for nothing really passes away
but rather passes on"*

the daughter wondered intently

*"passes on?
but to where?"*

her father raised his hands in the air

"to the great beyond"

216

we're drowning
in information while
thirsting for knowledge

may discrimination aid us

...

projection
is a weapon
used as a means
to a fraudulent end
by those who revere
playing the role of projector
misdirecting those they
have contempt for

...

spirits sanitized
hearts polarized
minds desensitized
shipwrecked mankind
adrift in modern times
terrorized by advertised lies

217

meditation
is the medication
of salvation

…

prayer
is a boundless ocean
of eternal devotion

…

is not that which is
indescribable and inconceivable
only receivable when the spirit is reachable?

so it is as
The Word's unbroken line
of Theophanic manifestations
from the beginning unto the end
of all ages and time

218

nothing ever is as it seems
once illusions split at the seams

...

sometimes it's best
to keep your utterances
to a minimum at best

*so it is said that they who know
tend to keep it all in their head
and that they who don't know
just can't wait to spread
all the nonsense they've
been fed and by led*

...

nothing
is nothing
and no-thing
for from no-thing
arose nothing less than
all things out of nothingness

219

what's the point of rules
if rulers can overrule them
at any point they choose?

...

leaders who disobey their own laws
disqualify themselves from leading at all

...

seek not to blind thine eyes
for the pacifying guise of pandering lies

...

escapists
are lost amid
the mirages and mazes
within the matrix

...

indecision
is damnation in
the form of inhibition

220

may you be
as a candlestick
sharing your flames
sacrificing your light
to spark another's wick

...

may you
rise above the
lows in your history
utilizing lessons learned
to make the most of your liberty

...

be not upset
in being misunderstood
by those who wouldn't
make the effort to
understand you
even if they
could

221

the cost
of free-thinking
is anything but free
one must be
prepared to pay
with relationships
from friends and family
with understanding
from culture and society
taxed to the edge of sanity
it's just the price offered
and debt owed to
individuality

...

when the world says go
the spirit says wait
what the spirit says love
the world says hate
what the world says think
the spirit says why?
when the spirit says feel
the world says deny

so who will you listen to
throughout the days of your life?

222

the mainstream conversation
projecting from news stations
traded integrity for insanity laced
with spitefully disingenuous
authoritarian emanations
ripe with disinformation

...

fake news
flows into bedrooms
with euphemisms to induce
psychological trauma in the form
of dread bathed in bastardized proof
attempting to manipulate all who view
into accepting lies and a life lived untrue

...

in this age of mass deception
laughter is the most potent weapon

...

in these times of universal tension
peace is the most vital dimension

223

when something comes between us
and once opened hearts close up
what we truly confront are but
our own buried obstacles as
inner flaws caused to rust
which petrifies the love
naturally springing
forth from each
of us

...

those who refuse
to ever adapt or add to
their worldview
see only the world which
their pride wishes
to pridefully
view

...

see that what we are
and what we could be
are as distinct as
the stars to
the sea

224

why do you choose
to close your mind and hide
when wherever you are
it's always yourself you'll find?

…

no matter where you go
your soul forever follows
as the hallowed abode
of the Spirit's holy
throne

…

the real dwells
beneath skin-deep appearances
and shallow temptations that sell
as pure waters aplenty
rest deep within each
of our soulful wells
only there being where
the profound is found
and true sustenance
felt

225

the most glorious sun
heedless minds can't perceive
is the cosmic luminosity quickening
the stars camouflaged as none other than
you and me

...

you admire too fondly
the stars luminescence
to ever be petrified
of darkness past
or present

...

in the spaces
between our words
are hymns to unity unheard

226

there are those among us
whose happiness rests
on making others just
as unhappy as
themselves

...

even if
the perfect society
could perfectly be built
it would remain unacceptable
to all those spiritually unfulfilled

...

mass-media culture
is but a cult of consumption
organized by vultures

227

intelligence is indifferent
to commercialized opinions

...

the fanatical fancy for fame
is a virus and vice all the more vain

...

the unprincipled pursuit of power
is as the locust whom devours

...

the excessive lust for luxury
will net little except regret and agony

228

our spirits
are free to briefly wander
throughout the endless
but upon bodily end
most begin again
while few attain
an unending
admittance

such is the repetitious rhythm
betwixt realms of existence
and degrees in sentience
in which all spirits must
by their own experience
reach an awareness of
the one and only
Quintessence

...

fire to light
illuminate the hidden
by love may we listen
to Oneness the Musician

229

criminality and corruption
are as blood thinner bleeds
for as they continually seep
so the consequences
continue to
increase

...

revolution becomes
an act of necessity
when despotism begins
to infiltrate everything

...

injustice
intentionally institutionalize
makes revolution
automatically authorized

230

just as
the athlete loses
their competitive rhythm
when they play down
to their competition
so to a believer
loses their faithfulness
when they lower their beliefs
to fit a culture of waywardness

...

constantly busy
never becoming
never being
constantly running
constantly trying
never fulfilling
how long until
you break the mold
and shatter the ceiling
keeping you caged in
disquieting dealings?

231

when some dream
they see visions and vistas
of what they in
their individual lives
could verily be
and do so with
zeal and impunity
but then why
when they wake
do they act procedurally
with apathy
at times
more mechanical
and automated
than a machine
remiss of onus
as if they never
dreamed in
the first
place?

so you tell me
who's more asleep
the waker or dreamer?

232

the phoenix within
soars and ascends
even amid the
most violent
winds

...

as birds of a feather flock together
so to spirits of believers greet in the ether

...

cellular division is a euphemism
for all arose in the image of
one Wisdom

...

as Spirit inspires
by Incarnating itself
so to cells multiply by
dividing themselves

233

confidence is certitude
of its competence

…

balance blooms
from forgiveness and fortitude

…

habits are perfected
when persistence is practiced

…

numbness is a result of
incessant lies and broken promises

234

it's sobering to not know
how little we don't know

…

if the unknown is ours to make known
then what higher power could one wield than this?
pulling back the veil over which all knowledge exists?

…

the greater knowledge we attain
the lesser understanding that remains

…

see that those gifted
the gift of understanding
understand that the gift is
not unfailing understanding
but in trusting unfailingly
one's faith upholding
the bridges forged
where once walls
were standing

235

no outside force can prevent us from rest
faster than an inner focus on forced expectations
we force ourselves to rashly accept
and restlessly expect

...

fret not over fickle futures
for one will arrive always on time
when you do
guilty secrets of deceit and pain
will destroy you in a day
over and again everyday
slowing eroding you
in every possible way
but innocent secrets of love and play
will reward you every day
by allowing you to enjoy them
without the sharp tongues
and judgements so smug
from others who refuse
to ever get to know
the real you

236

absolutely
all oppression
and every persecution
is but an aggression against
the One Absolute

...

the Source and its outlets
vary only by degree
and impressions
of distance

...

the world of stuff and shape
exists only by God's glory
and The Word's grace

237

existence is purpose
purpose is existence
anything more is but
superfluous noise
in the distance

...

consider:
there is no universe
unless there's a
'*u*'

...

the universe as nature
acts out its nature
through our
behavior

238

the resurrection of dead religion
to a renaissance of living spirit
is primed within us imminent

...

ancient paths of mysticism unlock rest
as modernity consumes to exhaust
delude and depress

...

a spirit electric
purged of desires
pure in detachment
a most heavenly magnet

...

if you
always do
your absolute best
in the end the
results should be
absolutely irrelevant

239

copious uncertainty
plenteous opportunity
novel crisis created
solution engineered
conspirators aplenty
obedience revered
twenty-first century:
advertised fear
corruption cheered
a new abnormal normal
forced upon us every year
like when authoritarian winds
manipulate the atmosphere
with coercion on the horizon
still the choice remains clear
for the free remaining among us
will never adhere

…

one who
goes against
established opinions
always faces the wrath of
the establishment's minions

240

notice:
do not be confused
for it is those most consumed
in the vacuum of ego's fumes
beneath pompous costumes
but always mainstream approved
who're paraded before me and you
in the hope our eyes will be glued
to the nefariously scripted views
while elite's prepare our spirit's tomb
and attempt to induce liberty's doom

...

infiltration over invasion
is a treacherous operation
weaponizing information
in order to control
the mind's every
persuasion

...

those who demand unquestionable participation
desire naught but unambiguous capitulation

241

consider:
these times
when free thinkers
are in such short supply
because all these haters as erasers
are ever so eager to cancel or crucify
anyone or idea that fails
to ideological pacify
their dogmatized
minds

...

it's far easier
to criticize than it is to create
which is precisely why the haters
can't help but hate

...

the ultimate futility
is attempting a conversation
with those who lack honesty or civility

242

those who readily accede to
their emotions emotional reign
are as prisoners imprisoned
in self-made chains

...

superstition and fanaticism
hitchhike along faith's mental mile
until discernment and discriminations'
decisive arrival

...

decisions are discernments
displayed decidedly
in deeds

do diligently

...

teachings are
tested in temperaments
exposing truth from tall tales

trek thoughtfully

243

zealous fear and hope
are opposite ends of a lassoed rope
with each loop eagerly awaiting
a throat to choke

...

in this material state
we either bless or curse our personal fates
based on the decisions we day to day make

...

potentialities and probabilities
together ripple into palpable certainty
by the conscious agency of conscious agents

...

there's nothing sweet
about the sweet nothings
governments whisper to us
hoping we'll remain asleep

244

some confuse
moral superiority
for mob popularity
when merely parroting
their chosen authority
virtue-signaling to substitute
for a vapid personality
with buried insecurities

...

the far fringes of
the latest rabid trend
to be outraged and
irrationally offended
at nearly everything said
is not just the cancel culture
it's the *cancer culture*

...

those who mold and own their own opinions
stand afar and apart from their culture's
conventional conventions

245

art is passion personalized
and personality magnified

...

bound beneath
the veneer of all art
are enchantments cast
from an enchanted heart

...

artists beyond time
make widows of us all
for we yearn for them most
only after they fall

...

the artist that is entirely understood
has misunderstood art entirely

246

reason exists in a fluctuating field
rebelling and accepting reality's reveals

...

brutes and buffoons
indulge in rebellious games
meant to outwit their mortal fates
to the dismay of naught but they

...

consider:
if even angels rebelled
knowing sure as hell damnation
just to experience a mortal probation
then surely the glory that is
the human temple
is of the most coveted stations
amid the whole of temporal
creation

247

correction
leads to progression
in only the progressor
who accepts being corrected

...

you're never in the wrong
by admitting you were wrong

...

why
put it off
for another day
when you can capably
take care of it right away?

...

why
try to fit in
with a society
fearfully inundated
in a collective psychosis?

248

even at its worst
it could always be worse

...

there's never not a silver lining
that's never not worthy of finding

...

half-full or half-empty
depends upon the one drinking

...

the collective psychosis
encroaching on our lives
is nothing less than
menticide

249

ideas have
a mind of their own
in that they choose
whose mind to
own

...

from ideas grown
cometh words sewn
unto acts shown

...

from ethereal realms
of thought cometh certain
symbolic letters to sanctified words
set in an assiduously alluring form
to alchemically transform
ideas that enliven
reader's inner
worlds

250

in some ways
to find the right way
we must get out of
our own way

...

the path to the way
and the way to the path
are within each self
passing through on
God's behalf

...

real love doesn't
require being said
real vision doesn't
settle for the win
real devotion doesn't
devote itself to clicks
real faith doesn't
celebrate the sin
real change doesn't
need an announcement
real death doesn't
end only transcend

251

are not the
wisest wisdoms in history
those which speak to us with
childlike simplicity?

...

do unto others
as thou would to thee

...

let thy deed be
as if thou were to receive

...

godly love
triumphs over
mortal life altogether
for it is born from a lover
prepared to offer up their life
so their loved ones can live better

252

unbreakable
is the heart that's bendable
and in itself dependable

...

a will unquestionable
is a spirit impenetrable

...

each individual piece
is a masterpiece
of the puzzle
complete

...

paralysis via contradiction
an all too human condition

253

notions we write and read
don't originate with we
but are indeed seeded
from the garden of
our connective
intuition

...

the spirit who
chooses not to read
is as a peacock who's
willingly clipped their wings

...

creation's
most hallowed vault
within the creative heart
is only unsealed through art

254

damnation is the distressed mind
descending into a depressive abyss
of torrential wrath and cataclysmic guilt

...

don't be surprised
by shady abusers and sly users
if you objectify your temple
to please shallow losers

...

when a dam breaks
and the deluge ensues
is when you'll discover
the most about others
but even more about
you

255

when push
comes to shove
one either capitulates in shame
or remains steadfast and overcomes

...

your potential
is a potential new you
to be or not to be
potentially
pursued

...

life
is a lovely
karmic dance
bodies move
hearts swoon
minds choose
souls advance

256

goals plunge into a forsaken abyss
when ambitions are abandoned
and the once ambitious quit
over the first signs
of the slightest
disturbance

...

plans
become delusional
when procrastination
makes laziness excusable

...

show don't tell
as actions unveil
empirical proofs
vastly eclipsing
rhetorical
spells

257

consider:
these are the times when
many
distract to divide
more
clamor to condemn
most
refuse to improve
few
dare to dream
fewer
yearn to learn
fewest
think to think

...

it could be said
almost all the torments
tormenting all our heads
are events which never were
or words which were never said

258

symbols
are forms of information
in formation
forming reality symbolically
far wiser than words
more ancient and dynamic
but only to those with
eyes inclined to find
and a mind untied
to investigate and seek
the secrets such symbols
keep

…

isn't it so
that even a nightmare
would be better than
never being allowed
to dream?

259

the only real privilege life gives
is the privilege for life to be allowed to live

...

the real war begins in the womb
just for the ability for you to become you

...

meaning
is the proactive activation
of conscious deliberation
but purpose is spawned
immediately when
one is born into
the world and
permitted to
rightfully
live

260

suffering
is the gift existence keeps on giving
so long as one remains existing

...

the hero
hopes not for hope
but knows their hope
is really a means to cope
when faith gets low and
needs be watered to grow

...

when all is said and done
don't be the one who
said they'd do
more than
what was
done

261

all this social media
and all we've become
is less social and
less trusting
of media

...

notice most
social justice
is only social
for the notice
and only just
for the corrupt
to overdose on
their ego's lust

...

if the world stays
heading in its current way
restricting another freedom
as if it's just another day
sooner or later everyone
will be forced to choose between
being a slave to the state
or an outlaw living free

262

a most virulent disease
undiagnosed most in our day
is the phantasmic dis-ease
we cause our minds
throughout the
night and
day

…

rash actions
produce reactionary reactions
leading to regretful interactions
unable to be redacted

…

we're being programmed to agree
with the notion that it's selfish
and socially unacceptable
to demand to be free

remember
no person nor power
can take your volition
without your decree

263

the strongest choose silence
the weakest force violence

…

as the rational build common ground
the irrational desire to burn it down

so it is
with empty cans
who when tossed around
tend to make the loudest sound

…

notice:
to zealously identify
is to intentionally cage the mind
into constrictive containers designed
to insidiously limit what can fit inside

…

more telling
are the eggs designated for internal dwelling
rather than the exterior basket used for bearing

264

immolate
imperious indoctrinations
inculcating infectious illusions
intent in imitating inner illumination

...

information
is as infinity
informing creation
of its infinite manifestations
in this matrix of amazement

...

isn't it odd
that some mock
the concept of a God
when all jokes aside
its far more likely
there's nothing
that isn't God
all the time

265

when unjust laws
are unjustly erected
reasoned disobedience
becomes justly granted

...

those who claim
immunity to criticism
are fluently versed in
pathological barbarism

...

hunters and monsters
act as one in riots
for opposites attract
when acts become violent

...

only in the perpetual now
are battles be won
one by one

266

laws
are not necessarily
lawful

...

justice
is not automatically
just

...

signs
are not necessarily
signaled

...

saints
are not automatically
saintly

...

compassion
is not necessarily
compassionate

267

notice:
the sleeping masses
would swifter sacrifice their rights
in the name of erroneous security
from fears designed to terrorize
than risk losing their vices of delight

*so it goes that those
who trade freedom for security
will end up safely enslaved
by those who orchestrated
the false need for the trade*

...

oneness *over* separateness

...

redemption *over* revenge

...

forgiveness *over* force

268

free will
is only as free
as one's ability
to act on what
they conceive

...

life is fair in that it's unfair

...

your wealth is as a gage
but worth is fixed innate

...

your soul is the treasure
your temple is its chest

...

it's quite possible
the impossible is quite possible

269

under the caviling skeptic's armored chest
are garments stitched of conceited threads

...

at what point does skepticism aggressively interjected
become truthfulness arrogantly rejected?

...

the real sickness
is not believing in
the sanctity of existence
and the unity underneath
true religion

...

virtue-signaling is the latest trend
made trendy by the unenlightened
desperate for validating attention
from echo-chambers which
enthusiastically praise
their submission

270

consider:
when some say
with sly serpent eyes
that time is money
they're lying
for *'time is money'*
it's just a phrase devised
by those who bought your time
with empty green faces
the carnal world enshrines
with just enough to stay
but not enough to quit
dive headfirst into debt
ain't it such a bitch?
save until your old
spend it when you're sick
come to think of it
what kind of life is this?
trading time for money
classic bait and switch
for bills they will reprint
but time is permeant
the present is a present
now is all there is
so if we know the cost
why are we wasting it?

271

choice
is as a handless blade
with no blunt end
two points sharpened
each of us wielding
some blindfolded
swinging thoughtless
others eye's naked
third one opened
to a path unfolding
each choice being
a meticulous cut
of destiny downloaded
those who ignore it
wound themselves
having not the training
nor desire to learn it

...

words become meaningless
when meaning neglects its purpose
purpose becomes heedless
when words lose their candidness

272

dreams from
the knowing tree
fall as opportunities
fruitful seeds from
God unto thee
all you've created
all you've surpassed
all you've become
all you've yet to be
all you've amassed
all you'll ever need
isn't it sweet?
the nectar of belief
sprouted by the grace
of faith watered deeds
apple of your eyes
love rooted deep
'come to me and
be ye complete'
sayeth the Lord
in soft echoes
sung in a
magical
breeze

273

reason
is unreasonable
to those who fan
the dogmatic flames
of their own delirium

...

listening is an evicted skill
in the ears of those inflicted
with fundamentalist pills

...

when ideology
is made the only policy
rationality is decreed
an irrational enemy

...

it's the first leap
that petrifies feet
till courage unreservedly
decides to dive deep

reason is to wisdom
what music is to rhythm

...

struggle is to success
what oxygen is to breath

...

if knowledge is a sword
then faith is a shield

...

motivation
only motivates the motivated

...

discipline
only disciplines the disciplined

275

well-being is to morality
what trust is to integrity

...

maturity is to responsibility
what dedication is to accountability

...

if harmony is a harbor
then tolerance is a bridge

...

beware of those who're there
yet unaware they're unaware

...

lucidness would be redundant
if opaqueness weren't so abundant

276

inscribed herbicide
to all illiberal thorns
planted as pernicious propaganda
which pollinate poisonous polices
and paradigms alike
is the potent poet's
poetic bite

…

potent poets
don't just blow smoke
with clever words and prose
they ignite cognizant infernos
via poised ink flows
and purposeful keystrokes
when the field of ideas
becomes overrun by
invasive ideologies
which soil
liberty's nurturing soil
and ravage the serene greenery
of free-thinking
autonomy and decency
for the weeds of
popularized groupthink
and doublespeak

277

consider:
if an end
your heart desired
were effortless to acquire
then there'd be no reason for
the desire to have ever conspired

…

you haven't given your all
until you have no all to give

…

obstacles make
achievements
possible

…

worldly eyes stare at you
spiritual eyes stare through you

278

gratitude
drives along
the highway between
what we think we want
and what we actually need

…

before any
action is acted
an idea is imagined
and an actor is attracted

…

if stillness is cause
and motion is effect
then death is an illusion
and consciousness infinite

279

notice:
a victim mindset
is a mind set
on believing in
the false premise
that it's powerless

...

the powers that be
impose force on you and me
to sacrifice our souls
and obey what
we're told

...

the real crime
is perpetrated by
the powers that desire
to oppress minds
with disempowering
lies

280

the best you can only ever exist
if effort is constantly consistent

...

when consistency is constant
progress becomes obvious
progressing constantly
as new results in
progress

...

the calligraphy of infinity
is the artist's epiphany

...

the will to create
is willed by fate

281

icebergs demonstrate
a higher assertion
in that fullness
can only be detected
by searching under
the surface

...

the only
coincidence
is the illusion
of coincidence

...

a cup's immediate usefulness
is on account of its prior emptiness

282

love guides
the heart's central compass
as a lovely lantern beaming illustrious

...

in nature's love we trust
for it's a love that refuses to judge us

...

the
heart is
most secure
upon realizing
then embracing
that which it is
readily willing
to sacrifice for

283

every time
you stumble on shaky ground
remember to center yourself
within the flow of the Tao

...

we may temporarily stuff our faces
with all the temporary stuff we wish
but they won't bring us any closer
to truly lasting happiness

...

sometimes
there's nothing we can do
to save a sinking boat
but we can be sure to learn
how to swim and float

284

knowledge
from nature and reason combined
can only be known with an open mind

...

it's impossible to reach a mind
that's vehemently closed
when by its very nature
openness is opposed

...

humility
soars with wings
able to glide over anything
the pompous world below brings

...

extreme pride
is the mark of a mind
extremely blind

285

notice:
gluttony and greed
metastasize disharmony
as neither can evade
the plagues writ in
selfish excessiveness
sooner than later
they'll crumble
any made sacred
inspiration dream
or steel beam
at the behest of
profit over everything
and egotistical *'needs'*
drenched in denials
and hyper-consumerism
so look closely
for the advertisements
puppet politicians and
vacuous celebrities
only really say
but one word
'obey'

286

it's not
the occupation one holds
but their motivations left untold

...

civic virtue
and social harmony
flow downstream from
tolerance of conscience
and individual morality

...

when virtue is all but lost
the virtuous must rise
regardless the cost

287

earnest expeditions
into the wilderness of mind
can feel as innocence lost
but in time are uncloaked
as the price sacrificed
for awakening's cost

...

awakening arrives
as a revivifying kiss from celestial lips
whose touch invigorates reason
to recognize one's immutable
divinity within

...

knowledge of the Divine
goes only so far as
the understanding
understood in
each mind

288

notice:
we are as ignorant
as we are conscious
for we can know nothing more
than our own conscience

...

the themes of our impressions
constitute the caliber of our expressions

...

only exponents of oneness
are sufficient in filtering out distinctions
by quenching the most conflicted souls
their yearnings for sure deliverance
from that bountiful fount of certitude
irresistible waters nourish and transmute

...

the travesty of tragedies
is when apathy overrides empathy

289

wisdom
is no longer wise
when it goes against that which
it knows to be right

...

they say
the most direct approach
is not necessarily the best
but wouldn't you
in most cases suggest
someone be blunt and direct
rather than lead you by a lie
so as not to cause offense
in the name of cheap respect

...

give gratitude unto
the falsehoods society provides
and tries to forcibly enshrine
for with every fable said
a hundred dormant souls
are arisen from
the dead

290

consider:
those who erroneously think
they must force others to think
exactly as they themselves think
never by their own will think
they just parrot what they think
is most popular to think

...

notice:
those who
have little to nothing positive
to ever say to you
happen to be the same ones who
are positive it's their duty
to be positively negative
about everyone else too

291

there are some in the present
whose presence is itself a present

cherish them

...

those who build you up
should never be passed up

...

we were *designed* divine

...

we were *created* to create

...

we were *born* to become

292

consider:
maybe the missing pieces
you believe you have to find
were never actually missing
only waiting for the right time
to reveal themselves to you
when you're in the right mind
to accept the unexpected
and expect acceptance
becoming one of your
most trusted guides
wise to remind
that the pieces
you long to find
were within you
the whole time

293

comfort zones
are self-imposed
premature tombstones

…

echo-chambers provide no rest
and cause the most needless of stress
in which most offenses and defensiveness
are caused by self-deceptions at best

…

why do you cling to that
which suffocates you?

…

distractions
thrive off distracting
the easily distracted

294

sometimes
the only way to feel alive
is to put the pedal to the metal and drive

...

a roll of the dice
can change your life

...

risk
is the kiss of life
when life really lives

...

notice:
at times just dipping
the tips of your toes in
is enough to right dive in
and never hesitate again

some things may never heal
but press ahead we must still

...

when a relationship
replaces happiness with woe
those in relation must be prepared
to let it go

...

how quickly
so it seems
do we cave to
perspective narcolepsy?
dazing and dozing
unconsciously conjuring
the most convincing lies
like we won't recall
all the simple times
simply spontaneous
as the most golden days
moments and experiences
of our lives?

296

if you crumble
are flimsy and mournful
from every miniscule
sting or prick
how will you ever
be able to withstand
those attacks
and injuries
most arduous
or drastic
some of which
tend to stick?
they key resides
in discernment
a lock fastened to
the door safeguarding
situational and
emotional intelligence
better known as
individual awareness

297

when critical thinking
becomes critically endangered
wisdom is deemed a pariah
and truth is made
a stranger

...

panic
is the toxin
which renders
common sense
uncommon

...

the essential common good
is that goodness
is common

...

the duty of our times
is to accentuate the kind
throughout all humankind

298

it seems
that nothing we see
is seemingly what
it seems to be

…

just because you can't see it
doesn't mean it can't exist
nor that it can't see you
to begin with
which means what we see
is less the seen
than it is the we
who do the seeing

…

only when thy mind
can no longer stomach
all the indigestible
and detestable lies
shall the Lord reveal
in sustenance of light
guides to nourish you
towards the true
and right

299

some spirits are fated to wander
until time expires and love retires

...

materialism is a prison
where cells are fashioned
according to the fashion
of the one imprisoned in it

...

darkness is not equal
brightness is not partisan

...

perhaps:
all of humankind
is unconsciously traumatized
by a cataclysm in ancient times

300

candidness
is the new influence
seeing that fakeness is so prevalent
even the frauds admit
it's evident

...

do more
expect less
say little
listen best
stay open
be blessed

...

simple
self-less gestures
are exceptional
self-full treasures

301

there are situations when
simply walking away
is the loudest reply
one could silently
say

...

ignorance is bliss
when the ignorant dismiss
their ignorance

...

there's a dignity in stability
only instability can perceive

...

don't give up
for everything given
gives you the ability to
spiritually level up

302

who are you
when there's no one around
to watch what you do?

...

find alone
your deepest truth
may be found in you

...

sometimes a simple *'why'*
is the most appropriate response
one could possibly reply

...

the notion of retirement
tells us to live our best lives
right before we expire and die
why?

303

the hardest part of letting go
is the nostalgia of that which
we used to hold

...

nostalgia morphs into pain
when the past is permitted to reign

...

personas pile up
when ego is left to judge

...

the biggest shoes
each ego tries to fill
are the expectations
we ourselves
instill

304

hell rages
in the everyday actions
which cause guilt and pain to swell

...

heaven resides
in the humble spirit
living consciously minute by minute

...

selflessness and benevolence
in the flesh
are as God's witness

...

narcissism and malevolence
in the flesh
are as satan acquiesced

305

you know you're free
when your beliefs
hinge on no one else
but yourself believing

...

trees don't
resentfully horde their seeds
instead they bountifully
let them loose when
they're ready

so it is with parenting

...

better to be
different around
everyone you meet
because everyone
is different in
fluctuating degrees
than to be continually
synthetic to no one save
your own spirit
underneath

306

failure is either
a stepping stone to grow
or a desolate dead-end road
depending on the approach
from the failure in control

...

failure never fails to prepare
those prepared to bear that they failed
to ascertain a new strategy for failings repair

...

unanticipated circumstances
unmask prudence and put patience to the test

...

every test is blessed

...

togetherness becomes an end
when mercy and compassion befriend

307

when one's lips are soft spoken
with a tongue seldom heard
you can be absolutely sure
that inside abides a mind
too expressive for
mere words

...

jealousy
is but the subconscious
made cognizant of
what it could be

...

a most slighted lesson
day by day deduced
is the invaluable value
of a daily pleasant mood

308

pay attention
to politicians who bastardize a crisis
by popularizing party lines
contaminated by lies

...

career politicians make a career
of compelling political opinion
to comply with selfish interests

...

political corruption
is undoubtedly entrenched
when term limits
are intentionally
nonexistent

309

love like a god
worship and adore it
love like a shaman
mystically explore it
love like a hoarder
savor it and store it
love like a sage
respect and implore it
love like a flower
nourish it to grow
love like a letter
open it to know
love like a vow
keep and protect it
love like a law
uphold and defend it
love like a tourist
celebrate the quest
love like a bonus
save it and invest
love like a volunteer
only if you want to
love like an infant
a heart brand new

310

perception has no reality
but the presumption of realities
hands have no feeling
but the sensations of feelings
eyes see no color
but the representation of colors
ears hear no sound
but vibration of sounds
tongues have no taste
but the impression of tastes
minds have no self
but the illusion of selves

so it is for those
who've learned how
to untether their soul
from their illusions
of old

...

the brighter fidelity
is forged from patience and sincerity
adorned in integrity

311

obscurantists operate
by obscuring facts
with emotional bait
meant to obscure
conversation and debate

...

observe:
the small things are everything
as miracles live in the minutia
of every precious minute
of living experience

...

consciousness is as perception
perception appears as reality
but what really is reality
if not consciousness
reflected back
at you and
me

312

there's a chance
that one's impartial stance
will feel as lonely as
a lost romance

...

the symptom of wisdom
can be as a poem
so lonesome

...

dawn still spawns
despite the dimmest of nights
and most demoralizing of times

...

never interrupt
an opponent
self-destruct

313

many demand obedience through an impartial guise
but did they forget mustangs refuse to wear saddles?
prayers ripe in digital pews and claim to empathize
but did you know god's of death love apples?

many smile in public when a lens is in vision
but did they forget the spectacle is a phantom?
conspirators parrot progress via televised division
but did you know despots love tantrums?

many search for truth in a vat of familiarity
but did they forget the universe is expanding?
insecure minds seek thorn bushes of popularity
but did you know the tree of knowledge is still standing?

many swallow synthetic drugs of distraction
but did they forget those pills are blue?
veiled puppeteers tug at strings of tribal passion
but did you know it's our consciousness they pursue?

314

the pacifist solution
to dissolve all illusions
is a disillusion revolution
turn off
tune out
exit the crowd
through a spending seclusion
an ascetic economic resolution
non-participation in its execution
against the powers and institutions
whom demean liberty as a delusion
rendering humanity to the subhuman

...

somewhere
through meadows
of sun-kissed flowers
and miles of old asphalt
at the feet of metal cages
resides a valley of hope for
the human race to transmute
into sages

315

the self
absorbed with itself
cares little for anyone else
unless them caring one way or another
benefits themselves

so it is as
so many in modern day
who adorn their ego in a golden display
foolishly unaware their idol made
is of foolish fool's gold
soon to degrade

...

the pride we
pridefully hide
is revealed most by
the responses we provide

316

though we walk as David
through the valley in
the shadows of *'death'*
with a certitude
we know and sense
even at our last breath
that death is simply
the most deceptive
but convincing of
fear-inducing
myths

…

death
is always smiling at us
cause it knows after breath
awaits worlds unlike anything else
we've experienced since we left
in the first place so we
could experience
another first
breath

317

sounds of a multitude
oneness in thought
creature of curiosity
understanding is sought
persona of turmoil
searcher of validity
heart of the artist
conscious lucidity
lover of wisdom
careful to attain
lips of nature
secrets of the brain
symphony of order
chaos to explore
lessons of life
failures to adore

318

notice how the sun
reflects off innumerable surfaces
in fluctuating grades and degrees
inspiring life through light
but it's still but one
heavenly body
ever bright
now see that our sun
is so much akin to you
a unique star
incomparable
to anything or anyone
shining upon
everything and everyone
but what shall
your light inspire?

verily
only you can determine
how you share your power

319

you'll discover
if you haven't already yet
that unless you become undone
from subconscious constructs
amid shadows sunken deep
or the many cultish cultures
saturated in consuming
even deafening personalities
so negative and weak
you'll remain imprisoned
destined conditioned
by the wishes and whims
of someone else's decrees
of who you should be

...

notice:
conspiracies gain steam
when lies become mainstream
now truth will indeed set us free
but not before we scream
wraths waxed in disbelief
at the stark scenes
now seen

320

we hear some say:

"why won't the world change?"

simply because
it is not first the world
but firstly each of us
that must internally change
our habits and ways
our desires and days
reevaluated
even remade
and rearranged
as rebirth and reform
are a cyclical phase
the music by whom
our instruments
play

321

love nurtures the field
wisdom sprouts as grain
gratitude swaddles the soil
knowledge falls as rain
flora and fauna frolic
awareness doth proclaim
though words fail to capture
the ideal remains

Thou art That
I AM
thy name
one and
the same

...

as threads are woven in a blanket
as pearls are strung on a string
likewise are all living things
bound to and united with
the Creator Supreme

322

within
the subtle heart of a tiny
outwardly insignificant
millimeter sized seed
resides the entire essence
of the mighty sequoia tree
only changing in degree
before it is planted
allowed to grow
and be
but why
should it be
any different
than you or me?
for although
we are small
once a seed
our hearts
are colossal
our nature
godly

323

we think
the Light irrelevant
until submerged in
a most bleak abyss
perhaps tis why
awareness surges
fiercest brightest
in turbulence
when existence
is revealed for
what it truly is
purposefully
purposed

...

if one can't
judge a book
by its cover
then how can
we so easily
judge one
another?

324

many know
that knowledge is power
but few know
the power of knowledge

...

the knower
the knowable
and the known
amid the unknown
rule upon
a single
throne

...

as the home houses the body
and the body houses the soul
so to the soul is the home
of the Infinite Whole

thank you for reading

may the aquarian age give rise to the ubiquitous sage

don bo byuti - nobody but i

Made in the USA
Columbia, SC
14 October 2022